HAL•LEONARD
INSTRUMENTAL PLAY-ALONG

AUDIO ACCESS INCLUDED

PLAYBACK+
Speed • Pitch • Balance • Loop

TROMBONE

Disney
Beauty and the Beast

To access audio visit:
www.halleonard.com/mylibrary

Enter Code
8226-6126-0524-8910

ISBN 978-1-4950-9615-0

Motion Picture Artwork, TM & Copyright
© 2017 Disney Enterprises, Inc.

Wonderland Music Company, Inc.
Walt Disney Music Company

DISTRIBUTED BY

HAL•LEONARD®

7777 W. BLUEMOUND RD. P.O. BOX 13819 MILWAUKEE, WI 53213

In Australia Contact:
Hal Leonard Australia Pty. Ltd.
4 Lentara Court
Cheltenham, Victoria, 3192 Australia
Email: ausadmin@halleonard.com.au

Visit Hal Leonard Online at
www.halleonard.com

ARIA

TROMBONE

Music by ALAN MENKEN
Lyrics by TIM RICE

BE OUR GUEST

TROMBONE

Music by ALAN MENKEN
Lyrics by HOWARD ASHMAN

BEAUTY AND THE BEAST

TROMBONE

Music by ALAN MENKEN
Lyrics by HOWARD ASHMAN

BELLE

TROMBONE

Music by ALAN MENKEN
Lyrics by HOWARD ASHMAN

DAYS IN THE SUN

TROMBONE

Music by ALAN MENKEN
Lyrics by TIM RICE

EVERMORE

TROMBONE

Music by ALAN MENKEN
Lyrics by TIM RICE

GASTON

TROMBONE

Music by ALAN MENKEN
Lyrics by HOWARD ASHMAN

HOW DOES A MOMENT LAST FOREVER

TROMBONE

Music by ALAN MENKEN
Lyrics by TIM RICE

THE MOB SONG

TROMBONE

Music by ALAN MENKEN
Lyrics by HOWARD ASHMAN

SOMETHING THERE

TROMBONE

Music by ALAN MENKEN
Lyrics by HOWARD ASHMAN